Alisha Nickole
JesusJuiceLLC
804-517-3254
Amelia,Va

Dedication/Acknowledgments

This book is dedicated to the light of my path and creator of all things within GOD, the foundation I stand on, my parents, Anissa Trueheart and Steve Nash, Delice and Roger Wingo (godparents) Mr. and Mrs. Deskin, Barbara Green Yarborough, Mr. and Mrs. Yarborough the anchors of my heart, my children and siblings, Anais, Jayden(godson), Justice, Keira, Terry, Tyree, Nicky, Kamaria,Tyree(Arviet), Rakeem, Avery, Chanelle, Tabitha, Marquell(Kesha), Wilyum, Clayton, Larry, Chris, Terrance, and R.I.P Erin Enia Deskins.

To the motivational wind beneath my wings Apostle Tara Owens and her husband Toney Owens thank you for your wisdom and guidance through the storms I have faced. Thank you for encouraging me to never give up on my dreams and to finish this book.

To Terry the love of my life for teaching me that LOVE hopes all things, bears all things, and believes all things are possible. No matter where you are you can't hide from true love it always finds a way.

And to Mrs. Lamay, from Yorkshire Elementary, thank you for giving me my first notebook, you knew before I did that I had a gift and I thank you for nurturing it.

Table of Contents

Introduction:

Notes of A Lost Angel: poetry edition is my hearts letter to our creator. It is the first of a series of books coming soon. In this life we often find we lose ourselves. On our paths through this journey called life, there is no guarantee that we know anything. We often find that the best place to look when you are lost is to the light within. Notes of A Lost Angel is about keeping a relationship and open line of communication with whom all light flows from. It's about taking the darkness that tries to consume you inside and shining that everlasting light on it. These modern day poems are an expression of heart and all the things that come with having one. These poems are from a collection of life lessons that I have learned. They contain all that I have faced in this journey we call life, and writing them gave me the peace I needed to face another day. Each poem is a representation of a groundbreaking moment in my life. Each one tells a story, tells my story of how being lost gave me an opportunity to search within myself. These poems were the beauty for ashes I found within.

It has been a long road since the day he said over me "let there be light", and I opened my eyes to this strangely amazing atmosphere we call Earth. Now, I have spent 946,080,000 seconds on this planet and I have come to realize in that space and time, I still have barely scratched the surface of finding out what this world we've found ourselves living in is all about or, more importantly what my life is all about. Truth is we all are searching, hoping, and striving for something. Some seek peace, love, and joy, some seek wealth, wisdom, and power, and some (those who I closely relate to) want it ALL!! Now I have spent a vast majority of my life doing all I could with whatever I was given to accomplish the task of having it all by any means necessary. I found on this road that has chosen me, that we are but a sum of calculated decisions that were first made by those in influence over us when we were being trained to grow, then added to all the decisions we've made in reaction to that growth. For me, I know I have spent far too long reacting to that growth and i soon found myself counting how many seconds, how many moments I wasted barely being able to tell which way is up because I was still reacting and not acting on what I had come to know from that growth. Every moment if analyzed properly will show you a lesson or blessing, is what a great woman once said to me. It means that you can take anything a tragic heartbreak or a terrible decision and find its purpose. You can find it's meaning when you remove yourself from the emotional stigma of that moment in time and you can grow as you learn and see that all things work together for the good, ultimately. I know you maybe saying to yourself, well you just don't know my story I mean I was raped, or I was abused how can that work for my good?!? See, I could go into the normal textbook spew of what doesn't kill you makes you stronger, but the truth is sometimes what doesn't kill you doesn't make you stronger it makes you bitter and angry, or perhaps even ashamed. Yet, the truth is in some situations the good we get out of it has nothing to do with us, but everything to do with how we help others who may be facing the same things. Sometimes we have to allow the light within to dispel the darkness in our hearts, come to forgive those who aren't sorry, and use the hurt as fuel to prevent that darkness from spreading to anyone else. It's a taking back of power, so to speak, when we say I am not a victim but I am victorious, because they gave me their best shot and I didn't let it break me.

Sounds hard I am certain it is easier said than done and has been a constant struggle for me as a survivor of multiple sexual misconducts including incest. But, I made a decision recently in fact that I am done reacting, IT'S TIME, yes the time is now to act, to take it all by the horns and say fuck you try harder next time buddy 'cause you will not stop my destiny. I can, will, and shall move forward, no matter comes my way. That is what this book is for me, that's what it means for me. I am taking all those reactions and turning them into action in my own special way. So thank you for stepping inside the heart of this Angel and taking this journey with me, this is ***Notes Of A Lost Angel: Poetry Edition.***

Destiny:

Destiny, What is our Destiny?!? Is it to run, to frolic free moving like the wind as it pushes the sea? Building empires of untold wealth? Building a legacy beyond ourselves?

Feeding life into something only we can see? Tell me what is Destiny?!? Do you really know?

I pondered this thing with all of my soul!! How do you know when Destiny's reached?!? And a still small voice came unto me as He called our dear mother home."Destiny is God's glory He gets when we make it home!

After all is said and done nothing remains but the love of the Son. So if you're still breathing there's still work to be done. Destiny is forever striving for the mark of finding your place in God's heart.

See Destiny is not a tangible thing and though it doesn't shine like a ring it brings riches untold and a boldness to your soul to know, that Destiny is nothing you can show yet you must find a way to tell the world that Destiny goes far beyond life's flurs.

See Destiny is within a secret place that anyone can find, yes Destiny is how you share God's glory so divine and when it's all over and they speak on your behalf your Destiny will be the only thing that lasts.

Butterfly, Butterfly:

Butterfly, Butterfly fly with me through the rugged mounts and across the seas, Through the deepest valleys, pass the highest trees, Butterfly, Butterfly please fly with me.

Butterfly, Butterfly lead the way into the brightness of the dawn's new day, into the shadow of the moon's favorite place to play Butterfly, Butterfly lead the way.

Butterfly, Butterfly it won't take long, sing to me your sweet wing song and we'll make magical music that sets us free Butterfly, Butterfly fly with me.

For You I Live, For You I Die:

In this Life we're born alone, but there's a place that we call home, and it's found in Christ our cornerstone, Brand new life and peace abound, listen to the secret sound He says:

For you I live, For you I die

Don't question it , cause I don't lie

Just open up and testify

For you I live, For you I die

Hung on a cross, Yet for you I rise

Yes pure love, don't wonder why

Yes time will pass and seasons will change yet

My love for you forever reigns down on you my love,

My precious child, can't go too far nowhere on Earth too wide

Just trust your heart where I reside.

Blind Living:

Martin Luther had a dream, I woke up to a nightmare of a cold stare, just another victim of a house where Daddy wasn't there or didn't seem to know how to care, So I hit the streets like a dog in heat searching for fulfillment in the endless beat of my heart being stomped by the world so cold, Tryna be the baddest bitch riding shotgun in the finest whips collecting chips of wealth on my shoulders and as I let each one dip into my hips in hopes to find love I only found the strength to get up after they'd nut and try again a shamed I swam so deep than deeper into my sin chased it with gin and a whole lot of indo but in the end though I found no peace as I look around at the generation and wonder what happen to us, what really happened to in GOd

we trust, freedom and equality, when now if I want to be somebody I'm trying to be white and if I want you to be a man and provide I'm a gold diggin hoe and you ain't no trick so you want get tricked into doing real man shit. We on a slave ship and we are the captains, when we lead our children further into the struggle with our rappin and trappin ourselves with nowhere to grow. Trust me I know I fell for the game myself gained plenty of bodies and a lot a wealth but when I looked at the reflection of myself I couldn't recognize my soul inside and I cried and screamed to the heavens I loudly screamed how could I have fallen so far from my dreams and how do I wake up and stop living blindly stuck

Nowhere Else To Go:

There's nowhere else to go when every right turn ends wrong, close friends have all gone and the ones left over are sick of hearing the same ol song. Nowhere left to be when you don't know who to call "me" cause all I have is countless yous of whose I'm supposed to be or which path is best for me. For ya see there's no wrong way to eat a reese's however it's hard to survive when you give yourself in endless pieces which are never returned from the men who left your sugarwalls drippin and blocks of self esteem missin. See I don't know if you listening cause I see you wondering why asking how could this be, why am I switching shit up... Well maybe you don't get me for I've said far to many times I love you and please be mine only to find defeat. See I gave and gave for love I was a slave and I admit you had me but as I've said before and I'll say once more There's nowhere else to go I say I want more and you say you're unsure so there's nothing left to see for you can't seem to commit to we much less me. Friends by day and Lovers by night, you always want to be single right after a fight so I always just tell you you're right but see last night while

you were gone I had another sleepless night and I ran to where I thought you'd hold me tight, but you weren't there and didn't bother to even pick up the phone like you don't care. As I lay bare in your empty space tears flowing as if they were in a race. I felt pain down to my core I went to sleep that way but I woke up wanting more than I was willing to accept before so there's the door and no need to return your key cause Ive changed the locks and lets make it clear I'm going somewhere other than here if you wish to follow I'd be pleased but if you dont its all the same to me for the next stop is HIGHER STANDARDS Ya see

Troubled minds:

If I were diabetic and my sugar was low, would you throw me down,

would you slam my head on the floor?!?

My guess is no and so I flow through these emotions and wonder when it became okay to lock me in,

Sure I may have sin, and saw hope only in the end but you couldn't begin to know what it feels like to declare war on yourself, when you're angry with the only one who can help within, immortal sin to take the breath that he gave you, a selfish move on anyone who really love you, yet you want to be free, free is all you desire to be from the things that drown out all your positivity as it

stifles all creativity and tries to divide you from the divinity

Only then could you relate but by then it's much too late, you've sealed my fate and you hide me from the world and I crave for the taste as I get lost in my own mind. Such a precious case of memories that have come and gone or stayed too long as they replay in my mind all day I watch as the earth fades away and I reach for strength to find my way out

I gotta get out, get out, GET OUT!!! Get strong, think quick, be wise, speak real, and don't ever look back for we're moving ahead pick up your bed.

Judge and Jury:

Im not perfect nobody who walks this earth is so

why you pointing out our hiccups

like you was perfect coming up, yea I fell down

so what may have made some mistakes but im

still getting up again

Im gon make MY OWN WAY

yea I know what you're thinking you know

what's best right?!?

Well Im sorry Im not with that and this is MY

LIFE

No disrespect I love you more than words can

say but I know the Lord he loves me so come

what may I'm going to be okay cause it's truly

not your way or mine It's truly up to the Divine

and everything Im going through was meant to

be and he knew

Yeah he knew what was coming when he made

me so how can you blame me?

Inside Out:

SUICIDAL THOUGHTS RUN ACROSS MY BRAIN AS THE
DEVIL WORKS HARD TO DRAG ME THROUGH PAIN AS
I TRY HARD TO TRY TO MAINTAIN I JUST CAN'T SEEM
TO OBTAIN A PIECE OF HAPPINESS AND EVERY MAN
THAT I LOVE OR KISS SEEMS TO DISS AND MY LIFE
AINT ISH THAT I WISHED AS A CHILD REAL DADDY
ALWAYS MISSING I'M ALWAYS FAKING A SMILE AND
ALL THE WHILE I'M BREAKING DOWN INSIDE
PRETENDING TO BE WHAT THEY CALL A SURVIVOR
AFTER LIAR AFTER LAIR FOUND THERE WAY IN
MEANWHILE THE DEVIL INTRODUCING ME TO SIN AND
I CAN'T WIN CAN'T GET AHEAD JUST SITTING HERE
ONCE AGAIN PRAYING I WAS DEAD EVERYTIME I TRY
TO RISE TO A BETTER SPACE IT'S ALWAYS
SOMETHING THERE TO REMIND ME OF MY PLACE AND
THAT'S NOWHERE I'VE DONE NOTHING WIT MY LIFE

EXCEPT BECOME A MOTHER B4 I BECAME A WIFE
AND NOW I GOT MY CHILD IN THIS STRIFE TRYING TO
MAKE HIM SEE A BETTER WAY WHEN I DON'T SEE IT
IN SIGHT AND I KEEP TRYING WIT ALL MIGHT TO JUST
LIVE AND LIVE RIGHT BUT RIGHT SEEMS TO GET YOU
LEFT IN THE DUST BUT I HAVE TOO MUCH HEART TO
GIVE UP AND SO IM STUCK BETWEEN A ROCK AND A
HARD PLACE PRAYING TO GOD THAT MY LIFE DON'T
TURN OUT TO BE A TOTAL WASTE YET IM LOOKING IN
THE MIRROR AND I HATE MY OWN FACE TRYING
FIGURE OUT HOW IM SUPPOSE TO WIN THIS RACE
WHEN I RAN OUT OF GAS BEFORE I COULD EVEN

PLACE CHOKING ON THE SMOKE COMING FROM THE HOOD WATCHING EVERYBODY ELSE PASS THE LINE LIKE THEY SHOULD AND THE CROWD STEADY WATCHING LIKE IT'S ALL GOOD AND ME I JUST SHED TEARS AND BEGIN TO WALK AS EVERYONE POINTS FINGERS AS THEY TALK ABOUT ME AND WHAT I'VE BECOME I SWEAR I'VE JUST GONE NUMB I'M TIRED OF THE STRUGGLE MAN IM JUST DONE TRYING NOT TO KILL MYSELF CAUSE I WANNA HEAR THE LORD SAY WELL DONE BUT LACKIN WHAT IT TAKES TO BE MORE LIKE HIS SON LOST IN A MERRY-GO-ROUND AND THIS AINT FUN ALWAYS FEELING LIKE YOU HAVE NO ONE THAT'S GOING TO STICK AROUND OR STOP THE RIDE CAUSE THEY WANT TO HOLD ON TO PRIDE WHEN TIME AFTER TIME YOU'VE PUSHED YOURS ASIDE I GUESS IT'S JUST THE WAY THE COOKIE CRUMBLES AND PLEASE BELIEVE I COULD CARE LESS ABOUT THE CROWDS MUMBLES CAUSE THEY DON'T KNOW WHAT IT'S LIKE TO BE STUCK IN THIS JUNGLE

Anais's Love Song:

Never thought I'd appreciate what it felt like to be late, but now I can't wait and time moves slow as you grow inside my soul

Your greatness is my goal as I behold my belly overwhelmed with you,

Know that I tell the truth, my greatest achievement will always be you, and through and through I gon do what it do so that you see your due and your children's children too, as they will grow in the love we've created as we build empires on the name of God's greatness no wait-list you ask and you shall receive all of the life I have inside of me, I give to thee wholeheartedly my love, my angel, my dove.

Mommy does love you that's for sure and no place, no mountain, no wave, no shore can separate us from our hearts as they beat in sync. It's never bye just see you later as I face this calling.

And yeah, I know it's hard to understand, and I cringe at every chance I miss to give you a good night kiss, and Know that no bliss seems high enough to achieve the warmth of your spark that, lit a new fire in the dark days I called my life and as I face this strife you are the silver lining and I promise you I will die trying to get to a place where I can give you wings to fly with.

Money Lies To Family Ties:

See Hebrew, money never changed me, excuse me, negro it changed you, cause suddenly pursuing our dreams wasn't good enough for you. I still love yes it's true, won't pop pills on hills, though for you, I'll look to them as I pray, and though you say we're through you and I both know that shit isn't true.

FOOL blood in blood out but we ain't sayin soowop, we just born of the same woman, the same man I AM YOU in a skirt it's true. How could you ever forget or sit around in your feeling if you felt some neglect, Negro don't lose your respect and open ya mind cause right now you're acting like a spoiled scared little child in the dark I mean you acting real blind and I can still remember when I held you for the very first time. Yea I dropped you but, it's fine you took it like a G and while you out here in ya feelings remember who basically raised you.

***Think about it?!?....*Negro when ma was at work who nurtured and saved you as they taught you the game. Now you trippin over money man this is just insane but I'm gon give you ya space but when you come to your senses just remember in my heart you're just like a son and yea I know you not my child but here goes lesson one money comes and goes but our soul is eternal and it don't profit you nothing to let it burn a hole in your heart cause I ain't drop it in your pocket acting like I owe you, Hebrew please stop it!**

Love Calls:

Inspire me, show me something new, give me show me something you

Love me, take me down the road to something blue,

Lead me, into the hidden mysteries of you and I am certain that will bring a lifetime of things to be seen and unseen between two beings who truly knew nothing other than to try

They say only fools rush in but you had me at hi, so don't say goodbye

I'm not sure my heart could take it, and although it's way too soon it's yours so please don't break it

We could make it through whatever together and whether you're on the road or home I'm your woman I'll be strong and hold you up never pull you down never leave you stuck and cherish each moment as a blessing as we learn our lessons of life

I hope you carry my heart into the position of your wife

Through all strife for better or worse as we both know that

Love can hurt we will push pass dirt and the pain of our past as we step out on faith and hope it lasts

We know there's nowhere to hide when loves calling your name and if you feel how I feel there's no need for games

Let's not live in vain or regret because I knew that we were something special the day we met.

Creator:

Creator, whether now or later there is no debate of your love for your children, No matter how we seem to rebel we're forgiven,

And I know we be trippin, got church on Sunday yet Saturday night we are in the club sippin, dippin, and blowin on that indo knowing that at any moment it could be the end yo

Yet you remain an everlasting friend, in spite of all the hurt we cause in you we can depend, you never hesitate to answer every call we send as you pick up fallen men there's no way we can pay you back

I hope you understand, take my hand Lord lead me home cause it's always you who comforts me on nights I feel alone

I'm too gone people try to say but I trust it's your love that guides me as I pray, I never stray from relationship cause if you took your love away tell me what could I do?

Although I may not always get it right I know I'm nothing without you!

Sunken Place:

Slippin Slippin this flesh is rippin my dreams apart and everytime I give in I'm right back at the start, twisted in the same web I weave and though I say I'll leave I keep coming right back, devil on my back screamin yeah I got that crinack and I'm right back in sin,

When the music's jumpin and the smoke creeps in to relieve your mind and they screamin yo just dance, take a chance party and look good, waste your days away, follow the latest silly trends and be the best, let the destruction of your soul be the way you achieve the arts and crafts of the finer things

Yelling money ain't a thing but I cling to what seems to be yet a dream of being royalty singing, dancing, praising in my father's house now realizing He's missin me because he never threw me out see I decided to leave in hopes of finding my dreams and things I don't need and yes I concede to the point at the end of the joint my soul still belongs to the KING of Kings and when i turn to him I will be transparent because I know He's there and has seen me through it all, watching me like a parent whose baby is learning to crawl and I know although I keep falling over all he wants to do is pick me up and help me start over

For when I cry out to Him. He won't leave me stuck in the pot for too long sometimes a fine stew must simmer in order to deliver the desired taste and when the time is right He will turn the page and like a star center stage I will transform the atmosphere with the power of the one who brought me here cause you see my fear is my only courage that I can stand here and still declare I'm worth it

For who I am in Him today is only because of His grace that I find myself still safe even in this sunken place.

Love's Hangover:

Hello Stranger, where have you been? Seems like a lifetime I've tried to let you in but only found the beginnings of many ends

Seems twisted don't it man and woman meet again in a world where he's become she and I'm not homophobic just wondering where my original love went

Is he now my competition in the club? Would he rather share my wig than my love?

Always wear a glove, when you are out of matrimony cause these niggas are faking and these rachets are phony and you ain't trying to make it home early just because it felt good not being lonely.

Somebody hold me through this bs cause I'm wondering where all the families went. Momma's out twerking, working, and never at home, and we all know Papa's been a rolling stone, who holds his own cash and gets plenty of ass or is back door smashing.

I'm not bashing I'm just asking what happened to tradition? Don't mean to sound old fashion but come on I'm not dissin I'm just wishing that a woman like me can find what she seeks

A man after more than just money, clothes, and being in and out of my sheets as he hits the streets or sneaking around with Tyrone.

I mean come on all the love can't be gone and I don't care if it's right or wrong see I have my own case to

answer for on judgement day and you're right it's your life you have the right to be gay but don't hide behind me be free and respect my right to fight for me and what I wish to receive!

A simple relationship between a REAL WOMAN and a REAL MAN! I'm no rachet gold digger so I don't need no thug nigga with six figures who thinks his dick's bigger than every man in the world and just to prove it he tries to fuck every girl in the world. MAN, I just want something real. So hello LOVE can you please sit your ass still?

Failed Fairytale:

I'm uncertain...

This is true,

Cause although the sting of your hands, the pain of failed plans and lost dreams have subsided

The wounds inside wear on and I've made myself stronger maybe too strong, for I feel divided

I know forgive and trust me I've tried it but how can we stand a house so divided?

Why fight it when we both see it's through cause you want to blame me and I'm not done blaming you

Such a shame we played the game rolled the dice and lost russian roulette and now we're in debt to this drama,

Now I've added a new man and you've added two potenitail baby mama's

Although I wish I could turn the hands of time perhaps a redo. I can't take back all the pain you caused or the things I did to you .

So fairytales don't always have a happy ending DO THEY?

Now I don't believe in one word that you say, So why stay?

Just sign the papers today and let's go our own way.

Love's Contradiction:

So wonderful I fell in love...

Now how do I get out?!?

See the honeymoon is over and my love is all poured out.

The courting is now finished, I'm stuck like glue yet reality has struck

He's Mr. Right now but he's no Mr.Perfect, we often fight even though it's never really worth it.

He comes up short, only gives to get by

I'm never put first yet I always seem to ride

I feel safe in his arms but it's there he makes me cry

I love him with my whole heart yet I often wonder why

For there is no logic to my madness,
no peace for my soul

When a love that was made for me is
being shared with the world.

Born Again:

The darkness fades as the sun kisses the night goodbye,

A new day dawns and I feel I can touch the sky.

Endless possibilities of what the day could bring dance through my head as I thank the good Lord I didn't wake up dead,

Instead He fed me new life and He's given me yet

another chance to get my life right!

Lost and Found:

Here I am once again,

UP in the wee hours of the morning,

Searching for direction in light, in the darkness of morning

Kiss hello and I still don't know so I guess I'll let these words flow fluently through my thoughts of what cost my life has brought,

WHAT COST?!?

I feel so lost on this search for abundance and so I do my unlimited joy dance through every bitter circumstance in hopes that I might see the chance to make it count

For when I add up amounts it seems to amount to I've gotten by, I've made it through

Fought through much struggle yes it's true and I'm still blue a tru issue I pray doesn't follow me to the grave this shit is driving me insane..

WAIT!! That was getting to deep, had to pause, rewind, and repeat all the same mistakes

Working out various outcomes as I beat my heart like a drum till it's numb

Got no feelings left inside on this ride, I'm throwing up my guts,

SIgns of the times, tired of giving a fuck, I'm stuck in this rapture like despair,

Suddenly a move in my heart

WHO'S THERE?

It's me as you and we both care, so please hang in there

Remade:

I can't be stopped

I'll give it all I've got

I'll give it all I've got

I can't be stopped

RIght here in your love dancing, praying, crying at your feet

It's where I belong it's where I am free

I'm stronger, yes STRONGER wait and see

A new day dawning CHRIST has remade me

I can't be stopped, I'll give it all I've got

I'll give it all I got, I can't be stopped

Surrender:

I thought therefore i was and am all that you see

I've felt the cold, darkness of night pull and drag me through the floor

Yet I forgot not your presence even when I acted as Gomer, a common whore as a I child I bore too many times too soon

Yet it turned out not to be my doom, just a blessing in disguise

And I thank you Lord everytime I look into those innocent eyes for I have come to realize that the suffering is a fruit, the pain merely a seed to bring forth the warmth of your juice filled with the healing I would need as I walked through the valley in the shadow of my sin, you still let me in and shone thy marvelous light on the situation

A guiding light providing a tunnel through this bull...

WATCH YOUR MOUTH, you know I'm your Father and this whole world is my house you're merely playing in the sandbox of my backyard

So just sit back relax and know in your heart I AM LORD and when the mean ole devil comes and pushes you off the swing know I will move Heaven and Earth just to relieve the sting

So bring your heart to me and worship in spirit and truth trusting and believing that I created this world for you and will see you through every single moment this is your life I've given you so

OWN IT!!

Even Me, I too Believe:

Why do I believe? How can I believe,

that His grace and His mercy is received when I know I've been deceived bit the apple just like Eve and enjoy the taste of forbidden fruit

How do I comprehend a love that I can never lose when I've lost love so many times

Tell me, who here knows the truth?

From the pulpit to the booths,

Tell me, who could ever choose?

What could ever show just how grateful I am to know, yes joy to know the truth of that light that leads me through?

Where you could love a sinner like me too!!!

Seasons:

Yes there are seasons that shall come to past,

Yes there are promises that were made to last,

But you can't rush the spring or tell the flowers when to bloom

Although the winters seem rough you have to go through.

So open up your mind learn how to play in the snow,

Let GOD in your heart, He'll teach you how to let go for He knows what's best, Yes what's best for you

Know seasons may change from summer to fall but God is in control of it all and if you only allow His son to shine you when bloom into the

beautiful flower that he has designed.

High Thoughts:

High thoughts I'm in my zone,

Lost on my own cost way too high to pretend I'm not gone with the wind

Bullseye and doves cry as I say goodbye to all the stress

Come way too far been way too blessed

Passed the test of time as I fell into a few crimes of my mind waging war against myself

With nothing but bitter tears and sweet silent prayers to guide me towards the light as I faced the darkest weary nights of my life

I fought for every breath that I've taken 30yrs in the making,

Seen enough fears to leave you shaking in the basement of a hospital butt naked let's face it we've all had our crosses to bare

We all share in some form of suffering but when we learn to let it go and trust in the King of Kings you soon come to find

He carried our cross and He laid down life true sacrifice

Now we'll never face it alone and best believe when we cry he feels every groan

So hold on you're going to make it through and when those haters come against best believe He'll fight for you

So stand strong and stay on the path He chose for you

And when the night gets long and it seems you're going to stray

As you light up that jay don't forget to PRAY!

Surely unsure:

I am sure,

Sure we will grow as we sow these seeds together

I picture you and me together exploring foreign seas enduring the weather and whatever tries to rage against this love,

everything that I can give just never seems enough and I know it gets rough cause I can't believe that it's you, could it be a dream love is here in clear blue

Yet my mind reviews like can this a nightmare within, fueling my suspicions blurring my vision of what's in front of me and I'm sure I've said it a thousand times that I'd move pass the past and forward with you love it's true

if only you knew I don't want to live without you but are you true?

Cause I've been here a time or two before

When love that I thought was mine ran out the door

And it left me on the floor of my heart, broken

so many questions unanswered so many words unspoken

just ran right through me after they rose in my bed and came to knew me

Now those memories haunt me and tear through the light of this love and poke holes in I love you and the broken trust you try to earn

I make it so hard to even though I know it's been earned

I don't want you to go I hope you can tear down these walls I want you to know

That I believe that this here could grow if I could find time to heal maybe one day I can trust this is real.

Whirlwind Romance:

It took six days to say I love you,

Six weeks to say I do,

Six months and we called it quits couldn't wait to say we're through

Not sure we can repair that which was left in such despair

And although I cry, I say goodbye as I embrace what is yet to appear

If I'm honest I do fear the consequences of my choices as I face those inner voices it forces me to think,

Have I gone too far? Did we move too fast?

Should I accept apologies? Can we move pass the past?

I think of shared laughs and shattered glass that slashed the pieces of my heart I never knew that after I do the real trouble would start

How could an angel break my heart?

I guess Lucifer was true cause he shined a light that was so bright I couldn't see the darkness in

you until we were through and now I wish I do could be undone and that was the end of husband #1.

Broken Vows:

Confusion breeds insecurities not sure which path is right for me

Lord guide me for I have to know, where my heart leads I have to go

So as it pleads to be free I pray that you've forgiven me,

A vow was taken yes it's true, I never meant to lie to you

Come way too far to turn around, spun soooo much guts touched the ground

Not certain what the future holds, yet knowing that my future's golden, it can't be stolen

So in spite of this pain of marriage failed, babies lost, potential withheld

I was always trust you to balance the scales for everything you do is right

Lead me from this darkness into the light, though the vow breaks and my heart falls I pray that it makes it into your arms.

Love Abandoned :

Today I thought of you

Did you think of me?!?

Of what our love has come to be,

A trail of broken memories

He said, she did so we can't be,

Yet we yearn for just a taste of we

The heat we bring between the sheets

A love so strong it cuts too deep to sleep or

Live undone when you're not with me

A crazy Bitch a Player of pride

There's nowhere to run now

Nowhere we can hide,

The years that passed along this ride

I miss you and though it goes unsaid I know you're missing me

And this season of war is killing me a battle I thought we'd see

VICTORY

Has become a plague in my heart

Can't see, only hope in evidence of

my faith in the man i know you can be

keeps me on the field of love can you see?!?

I wonder as time flies by do you even care

That we are both bleeding love

and will you ever heed to my need to be true to a

love that is only me and you or are we

through?!?

Though I am unsure I could never search for more

So I leave this open door in hopes that you will

Come and save me from my heart's floor because it's you and only

YOU I ADORE.

About The Author

AlishaNickole, has learned through many hard lessons one of life's great truths THERE IS NOTHING TOO HARD FOR GOD!!! She is a virtuous and victorious woman called to many great things including writing, singing, dancing, and public speaking. She is a mother, a daughter, a sister, and a genuine friend. Her aspiration in life is simply complex to tell the world of the story of how God always gets the glory!!

www.ingramcontent.com/pod-product-compliance
Lightning Source LLC
Chambersburg PA
CBHW040830050726
47507CB00021B/171

9780692175187